PIERRE MOREL

THE SIGHTS OF
CARCASSONNE

Translated by A.-G. Catford, M. A. (Cantab.)

*Illustrated with 41 heliogravures
and 16 quadrichromes*

Surveys by Pierre Embry
(Curator of the City Museum)

ARTHAUD

Collection

" *THE SIGHTS OF FRANCE* "

THE SIGHTS OF CARCASSONNE
CHÂTEAUX OF THE LOIRE
PARIS
SAINT MICHAEL'S MOUNT
VERSAILLES

With text in French :

EN BRETAGNE. CORNOUAILLE
EN BRETAGNE. TRÉGOR ET LÉON
EN BRETAGNE. CÔTE D'EMERAUDE
CARCASSONNE. LA CITÉ
CHARTRES ET SA CATHÉDRALE
LA CHARTREUSE - GRENOBLE - CHAMBÉRY
CHÂTEAUX DE LA LOIRE
LE CHÂTEAU DE VIZILLE ET NAPOLÉON
LA CÔTE D'AZUR
MOISSAC
MONUMENTS ET PAYSAGES D'ILE DE FRANCE
MONT SAINT-MICHEL
PARIS
VERSAILLES

By the same author and publisher :

CORSE
FONTAINEBLEAU
MARCHE ET LIMOUSIN
VERSAILLES

PRINTED IN FRANCE

CARCASSONNE

I. HISTORY OF THE CITY

The hasty visitor to the world-famous City of Carcassonne is charmed by its picturesque and romantic effect. Dominating the course of the Aude it presents an incomparably striking scene in the summer sun, or when winter sprinkles it with snow. The fireworks display which every year, on the night of July 14, kindles a thousand fires at its battlements is a grand spectacle.

For those who have time to linger and visit it in detail Carcassonne constitutes the most complete museum of the military architecture of the Middle Ages.

Each period has left its mark upon the City, from the fifth century, when the Visigoths applied to the original enclosure the principle of Roman architecture, until the sixteenth when the general use of artillery brought about a revolution in the art of siege. The traces of each period are as clear and distinct as geological strata in a section of ground.

In the nineteenth century, if there are grounds for criticism in the over-radical nature of Viollet-le-Duc's restoration — which in particular abolished the space arranged for guns — it had, none the less, the merit of completing the general effect handed down by the previous centuries.

THE CITY DOWN TO THE ROYAL OCCUPATION (1226).

Carcassonne is composed at the present day of two agglomerations, the lower town and the City, which the outskirts of la Trivalle and the Barbican join on the left bank of the Aude.

Nowadays the living part is the lower town which is broadly spread out in its alluvial plain, at the point where the road from the lofty valley of the Aude, coming from the South, meets the great highway from Narbonne to Toulouse; this knot of communications has brought about the importance of the town which has become a great wine market. When its security was assured, the ministries of the City migrated towards it, little by little, and even the clergy, isolated on their promontory.

Today the higher town is no more than a museum; the crowds of visitors give it momentarily a fleeting animation, but the life of older times has withdrawn from it for ever.

THE BEGINNINGS

It was not the same formerly. The soil of the City has been overturned too much in the course of centuries for prehistoric excavations to be made successfully there, but remains unearthed in the neighbourhood are too numerous for it to be possible to suppose that men of the neolithic and bronze ages had neglected this steep eminence, next to the course of the Aude. This spur, northern counterpart of the Corbieres, which a simple rising of the ground could isolate without trouble from the heights to which it is connected, seems predestined to be a camp.

The small town of Volces Tectosages, *Carcaso*, in the Roman epoch, never had an importance comparable to that of Narbonne. A Roman camp *(castellum)* probably existed there. It watched over the route which then ran on to the foot of the declivities of the City.

Forerunner of the present fortified belt, nothing remains of the small enceinte, and the supposed traces of its praetorium disappeared in the XVIIth century. Not one tower, not one curtain, in spite of what Viollet-le-Duc thought, and which is still repeated now and then, is built upon Roman foundations. Nevertheless, particularly to the north of this camp and as far as the road, houses crowded into the shelter of the fort; the discovery of a mosaique, whose date seems not later than the IIIrd century, under the courtyard of the present castle, outside the Roman enceinte proves the existence of a villa of some importance.

But the destiny of the City was to be a fortified town.

Turbulent times which gave full credit to its military importance, were those of its prosperity. When political issues and treaties altered the plan of frontiers, keeping them at a distance from the walls of Carcassonne, the town fell into a half-sleep.

THE VISIGOTHS

The great invasions, striking a death-blow to Roman power, induced the establishment of barbarian tribes. During the second half of the Vth century, the Premiere Narbonnaise (future Low-Languedoc) became the prey of the Visigoths which the Romans had intended to canton into Spain (412), their duty being to drive the vandals from the Peninsula. Without even having completed this task they crossed over the Pyrenees, made Gaul yield to them from the west to the Loire (419); in 456 they transgressed these limits, took possession in 462 of the Narbonnaise, of which Carcassonne was a dependence. Under King Euric I (466-484) they attained their greatest expansion, held all the country south of the Loire, even went beyond the Rhone and possessed themselves for a time of Provence. It was probably this king who constructed the most ancient enceinte whose remains we have preserved : numerous remains, since the perimeter of the inner enceinte blends almost exactly with that of the Visigothic town, whose towers and curtains have very often undergone, in the course of the centuries, no more than a work of restoration.

Much more extensive than the Roman *castellum*, the Visigothic enceinte included all or part of the agglomeration which had developed beneath the walls of the latter. Carcassonne thus assumed its new character and became, instead of a fort surrounded by an open town, a fortified town.

Base of operations for the Visigothic kings in their conquest of the Midi, Carcassonne was soon to take on the function of frontier-post which it was to have for ten centuries. Clovis, converted for the last ten years to catholicism, became the champion of the bishops of the Midi, persecuted by the Arian Visigoths. In 506 he beat these latter at Vouillé, near Poitiers. In a few months he possessed himself of all the territory south of the Loire and, according to the historian Procopius of Cæsarea, he was only halted by the walls of Carcassonne, whose siege he attempted in vain (508). From that time the Visigothic possessions in Gaul were approximately confined to the future Low-Languedoc, which took the name of Septimanie (present departments of Pyrenees-Orientales, Aude, Herault and Gard). This province was protected on the Toulouse side by the fortified enceinte of Carcassonne, bulwark of defence.

During more than two centuries of relative peace, the town developed, and overflowing the ramparts, a scion of the latter, the market-town, proceeded to spread over the north-west slope of the ridge, as far as the present Narbonne road. From that time, the Visigoths surrounded this suburb with walls.

When, imitating the shrewd action of Clovis and wishing to establish his rule which the duality of religions menaced (the Visigoths had remained Arians whereas their Gallo-Roman subjects were catholics), King Reccarede I (586-601) became a convert (587), it was in the market-town that he established the first bishop. The first cathedral, Notre-Dame, arose on the site of Saint Gracieuse, the present chapel of the Great Seminary, whose tall Gothic doorway is to be seen beyond rue de la Trivalle.

This agglomeration was later named : faubourg Saint-Vincent, or Petit-Bourg. This latter name by way of antithesis to Grand-Bourg or faubourg Saint Michael, a development of a fortified *castellare* which, from the IXth century was attached to it to the south and south-east, thus testifying to the increasing prosperity of the town.

The conversion of Reccarede had deprived the Merovingian kings, natural defenders of catholics against their arian neighbours, of all pretext of intervening in Septimanie. The inhabitants, however were not faithful to the kings; between 585 and 598, they twice opened their gates to King Gontran's army commanders which thus preluded a projected expedition into Spain. The defeat of his troops under the walls of the City made him give up this plan. Moreover Francs and Visigoths were soon to be reconciled in the face of the common enemy, the Arabs.

THE ARABS

Crossing the Straits of Gibraltar, they penetrated into Spain in 711; the country was quickly conquered, the Visigoths were driven back into the kingdom of the Asturias and into Septimanie. The invader put them to flight; in 713, he pillaged the town of Carcassonne and Notre-Dame cathedral. Repeating the exploits of the Visigoths two centuries before, the Arabs took possession of Narbonne between 719 and 721, and, no later than 725, Carcassonne was besieged and taken by assault. Just as the Visigoths had been by Clovis at Vouillé, they were overwhelmed near Poitiers (725) by Charles Martel, who stopped their expansion northwards, reducing their domain approximately to the Iberian peninsular, for Septimanie badly conquered by them, where they experienced a hard time with the Visigothic lords, now constituted a protecting bulwark. The possession of Carcassonne itself did not last for long. When, with the support of independent Visigoths, Pepin the Short, in 759, seized Narbonne, driving the Moors back into Spain, Carcassonne was freed from their yoke for several years.

THE CAROLINGIANS.
THE FEUDAL DYNASTIES

Under Charlemagne and his first successors, the frontiers of the empire were taken well south of the Pyrenees; Gothie or Septimanie ceased to play the role of rear frontier which then belonged to the county of Barcelona. The latter, and its dependency Roussillon, continued to be in the power, in theory at least, of the king of France until 1258. Under the Carolingians, however, the first dynasty of hereditary counts was established. At the beginning of the Xth century, Saint Gimer, Bishop of Carcassonne, transferred the cathedral seat from the town into the City.

In 1067, the counts of the first line were succeeded by a dynasty of viscounts, descended from the counts of Barcelona. Soon the Trencavel (Cut well), viscounts of Beziers ousted them and added to their title that of viscounts of Carcassonne. Under this dynasty, many embellishments in the City mark an era of prosperity. About 1130, the ancient castle supported against the Narbonnaise gate, was replaced by the more important one which we see today. About 1150 was completed the Romanesque cathedral of Saint Nazaire, whose nave is still standing. A fine episcopal palace was added on to it in the ten following years. At the same time, the development of suburbs, which came to encircle the enceinte on all sides, give evidence of the richness of the town.

THE ALBIGENSIAN CRUSADES. SIEGE OF 1209

The Albigensian war troubled all the first half of the XIIIth century. Putting an end to the feudal age, it substituted for local dynasties that of de Montfort, then the king of France himself. As under Visigothic rule then Arab, it was again a religious issue which enabled royalty to penetrate into these regions.

In the XIIth century the Cathares heresy, connected with eastern manicheism, had spread over the Midi of France, whence the name of Albigensian given to its votaries. In vain were peaceful means exploited to lead them back to orthodoxy. After the assassination of the papal legate Peter of Castelnau, Pope Innocent III had the crusade preached against them, and this was, under the command of Simon de Montfort, the invasion of the Midi by the nobility of the North of France. As it did later, for the wars of Religion, the conflict took on a character at once religious and political, the latter in the end prevailing over the former. The Count of Toulouse, Raymond VI, who held all the land extending to the far side of the Rhone, was at the head of the Albigensians, assisted by all his vassals, and amongst them the most powerful, Raymond-Roger, viscount of Beziers, Carcassonne and Albi. Besides their military forces, the crusaders had on their side the sympathy of the clergy and of a part of the population which remained orthodox.

The war broke out in 1209; after the sack of Beziers, the crusaders appeared before Carcassonne which Raymond-Roger had just prepared (1st August); but the place was poorly organized for defence. The two suburbs which flanked the City to the north and south had walls that were inadequate and too distant for their shooting to be supported by that of the fortress. Moreover, to defend these suburbs it was not possible to consider leaving too many combattants there as their presence might become indispensable from one moment to another, on the battlements of the City. Therefore it was by the attack of the Bourg to the north that on the 3rd of August Simon de Montfort began. In two hours it was taken and committed to flames. Upon its levelled site, engines of war were laid out.

On August 7th, after a vain attempt at mediation by Peter II of Aragon, the *castellare*, to the south, was likewise attacked. Mining having opened a breach in its wall, the defenders themselves set fire to the mass and retired into the City. People from the destroyed surburbs and the surrounding countryside were already filling it; famine began to make itself felt. Resistance became useless : Raymond-Roger surrendered the stronghold. It was subjected to harder conditions : the inhabitants were driven out of it clad only in their skirts and breeches, and the viscount, thrown into a dungeon of the castle, died there the following year.

On August 15th, the crusaders made their solemn entry into the City which Simon de Montfort fitted up and converted into an arsenal to make it the headquarters of his last campaign. The castles of the upper valley of the Aude were soon taken; Peter II of Aragon, brother-in-law of Raymond VI, who had taken his part, was vanquished at Muret (1213), and when in 1215 the son of Philip-Augustus, the future Louis VIII, came to visit Simon invested by Innocent III with the States of Raymond VI, the powerful vassal received him in the City where he made the figure of sovereign in the eyes of his distant suzerain.

The country was, however, ill pacified; in 1218, Simon de

Montfort was killed under the walls of Toulouse which he was besieging. His son Amaury inherited his possessions, but, of a weak character, he was soon to be discouraged by money difficulties and the troubles which the ancient lords of the country stirred up. In 1223, Carcassonne was likewise besieged by Raymond VII, son of Raymond VI, but in vain. On the 14 th of January 1224, Amaury de Montfort signed peace with his adversaries, at the foot of the City; he left the country, never to return. Four days later, despite the accepted treaty, Raymond VII installed at Carcassonne the Trencavels' heir, Raymond II.

In reply to this breach of trust, Amaury, incapable of reconquering his States, ceded them to King Louis VIII.

THE ROYAL PERIOD

In June 1226 the king accomplished the occupation of Carcassonne without striking a blow, the consuls having made their submission; he proceeded there in person the following September. In 1229, the treaty of Paris putting an end to the Albigensian war, brought into the royal domain the greater part of the States of the Count of Toulouse; from then on Carcassonne never left it.

CONSTRUCTION OF AN OUTER ENCEINTE

Henceforth the City was the seat of a royal seneschal responsible for administering the recently conquered countries.

In the first place he applied himself to reinforcing the town's defences in accordance with the new principles of fortification. Between 1228 and 1229 a line of lightly built ramparts was raised around the Visigothic enceinte, on a site very close to the present outer enceinte, if not everywhere identical, except to the south of the Narbonnaise gate where these walls, deviating about two hundred metres from the present line, annexed a new quarter, built upon mount Saint Michael, in the place now occupied by the cemetery and beyond. On the opposite side the outworks of the Aude barbican, on the site of the present Saint Gimer church, facilitated access to the banks of the river. Finally, this new enceinte, fortified with towers, consisted of three semi-circular barbicans, commanding the principal gates and posterns, on the approximate site of the Saint Louis (Narbonnaise archway), Notre Dame (Bourg doorway) and Cremade (Saint Nazaire archway and du Razès postern) barbicans.

RESUMPTION OF THE ALBIGENSIAN WAR. SIEGE OF 1209

More and more was the City occupied by public buildings, dependencies of the bishop and dwellings of knights and royal officials. The mercantile population was relegated to the suburbs the reconstruction of which had not been delayed; that to the north, the ancient Visigothic town, had even re-erected its walls.

Such was the condition of the place in 1240 when Raymond Trencavel II presented himself before the place after having assailed and conquered in a furious skirmish all the surrounding country where he still had some supporters. The Bourg was surreptitiously delivered up to him by the inhabitants, who were loyal to their former lord. About thirty priests whom the incident had taken by surprise, and who had taken refuge in Notre Dame church, were massacred there by the populace (9th september 1240).

From the Bourg, Trencavel occupied the other suburbs without striking a blow thanks to the complicity of the inhabitants; on the 17th September he attacked with a mangonel the Aude barbican which was fortified with a stone course, but he failed. From the cellars of the nearby houses seven tunnels were then driven up to the outer enceinte. All were countermined, and the besieged repulsed several attempts at scaling.

In the night of 11th-12th October, menaced by an army sent to the help of the town, Trencavel raised the siege of Carcassonne and retreated, followed by a party of the inhabitants of the Bourg. This was his last attempt. Some years later he made his submission under the terms of which he was bound, together with his principal supporters, to accompany Saint Louis on the seventh crusade (1248).

Seneschal William of Ormois had personally directed the defences of the stronghold. As soon as the siege was raised he busied himself in essential repairs.

The besiegers of 1240 had utilised the houses surrounding the city to screen their movements as well as to establish their mineheads. By means of duty service levied throughout the country, d'Ormois had these suburbs demolished, including the old Bourg to the north. Thus their heresy-ridden inhabitants, supporters of Raymond Trancavel II, were punished and the approaches of the stronghold were cleared. Deprived of their dwellings and outcast, the townsmen were amnestied in 1247 whereupon they installed themselves in the place where low Trivalle quarter stands today, beside the Aude; then, between 1260 and 1262, they passed over to the right bank and created the present low town.

From 1240 the royal engineers organised the defence applying the new principles of military art; a citadel, raised up on open ground, formed by two lines of concentric walls, the outer enceinte being everywhere within bow-shot of the inner enceinte.

The line of the outer ramparts of 1228-1239 infringed this principle, to the east, where mount Saint Michael constituted a bulge. The magnificent keep known as the de la Vade tower was built apart in 1245. Its purpose was to provide views from this narrow spot to beyond this original outer enceinte. About ten years later de la Vade tower was connected to the new outer enceinte. Certainly begun before 1256, — the date when the administrators of Saint Eloi hospital were reclaiming the price of the stone from their ancient building which had been used in the new fortifications, — these walls were probably finished in 1260, in much the same state in which we now see them. In 1259, at all events, Notre Dame barbican was in existance. On examining these walls one notices, in the curtains on both sides of each tower, traces of joinings in the masonry. This detail makes us suppose that the original towers alone were demolished and replaced by the present towers, without doubt stronger, which were carefully joined to these probably more ancient curtains, which we suppose to have been erected between 1228 and 1239.

In order to hold in awe the inhabitants, still suspected of heresy, the Inquisition became established at Carcassonne; from 1240 to the middle of the XVth century, sometimes oppressive and with repeated use of the stake, then more tolerant, the tribunal with the ominous repute repeated its investigations and trials. The round Bishop's tower, wrongly called of the Inquisition, at any rate was never used by him as a jail; in 1258, the *wall* (as the prison was named) was built at the foot of the City, below the square Bishop's tower.

Engaged in restoring its ruins, Carcassonne enjoyed a peaceful existence until the end of the reign of Saint Louis (1270). When work on the ramparts was finished workmen and architects from the North applied themselves to embellishing Saint Nazaire cathedral; about 1263 the chapel of Radulphus or Razouls was built; in 1269 the magnificent Gothic choir was begun, in the style of the IIe de France.

PHILIP III LE HARDI (1270-1285)
CONSTRUCTION OF THE SOUTHERN SECTOR AND THAT OF THE NARBONNAISE ARCHWAY

The reign of Philip le Hardi (1270-1285) was as prosperous for the City as his father's had been. Seat of a seneschal's jurisdiction, it maintains the same administrative activity; but in the pacified Midi, henceforth assimilated into the kingdom, it no longer had for its primary mission the surveillance of the neighbouring country. The City became a frontier post and played an important role in the war against the King of Aragon, Peter III. The latter, instigator of the Sicilian Vespers (1282), disputed the kingdom of Naples and Sicily with Charles of Anjou, brother of Saint Louis.

Carcassonne was not only an arsenal where troops completed their stores; the king of France perfected its fortifications; he erected magnificent works of dressed stones : the Narbonnaise gate, the Treasury tower; from about 1280 to 1287 he constructed the southern sector of the ramparts from the tower of Justice exclusive to the tower of the Prisons.

Between 1255 and 1260 approximately, as we have seen, the outer enceinte had been built as it appears today. Next to be undertaken was the levelling of the *lists*, the space included between the two lines of walls which, by the lay of the land, had a steep slope from the inside down to the outside. Levelling took place; this work uncovered the Visigothic foundations of the inner enceinte — they were shallow and did not reach the rock- and even laid them bare so well that this bed of masonry, formed of courses of mortar and rough stones, is visible today a few yards from the wall of the lists. Viollet-le-Duc mistook these foundations for remains of Roman constructions.

Another consequence of this levelling : the soil, inside the City where numerous deposits of earth had been made in the course of the ages, became raised and exerted a pressure on the walls. To their pressure was added the weight of the Visigothic towers, with their solid bases; the solidity of several of them was compromised, some even leaned outwards.

This defect the architects overcame by economical means no doubt provisional in their ingenuity : the waiting stones propped up against the curtain nearby, to the south of the Narbonnaise gate, testify to their intention to rebuild the fortified enclosure of this sector. Meanwhile they built an underpinning wall beneath the Visigothic foundations. It was intended simply to add to the general firmness and is visible from here on in facings of the curtains and towers.

When, moreover, they underpinned the high parts of the edifice, the Visigothic construction, characterised by its small sized stones mingled with brick courses, looked like a horizontal band more or less wide, running between two courses of XIII century masonry, — recognisable by its larger sized stones (period of Saint Louis), for the sector which runs from the castle to the Constable's Mill tower inclusive, in dressed stone (period of Philip le Hardi — Philip le Bel) for that which goes from the Narbonnaise Gate excluded to the Saint Martin Tower excluded, — which — frame it above and below (See. scheme, above).

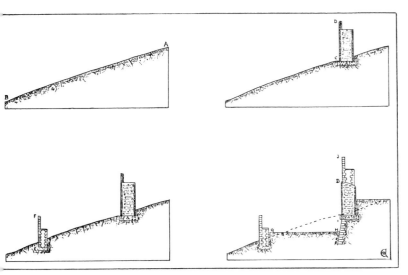

UNDERPINNING OF THE VISIGOTHIC FRONT
AND LEVELLING OF THE GROUNDS IN THE LISTS.
DIAGRAM BY PIERRE EMBRY.

A. B. Original lie of the land. — C. D. Visigothic curtain. —
E. F. Outer enceinte. — G. H. The lists after levelling. —
H. I. Propping up. — D. J. Rebuilding of the coping.

THE CITY, FROM THE XIV CENTURY TO
THE REVOLUTION

The works commenced under Philip le Hardi, who died
in 1285 on his return from the disastrous crusade to Aragon, were
finished in the first years of the reign of his son and successor
Philip IV le Bel (1285-1314). Their completion marks the archi-
tectural zenith of the City; it then appeared very nearly as it
does today.

But its military importance diminished considerably.
The attention of the monarchy was directed towards other

regions. The main theatres of the Hundred Years' War were the north and south-west of France; the City's role became episodic : it remained the arsenal on which the officers of the king of France drew for their campaigns in Agenais or Gascony. At the most it saw marching past beneath its walls, but out of range of its shots, troops of infantry and the army of the Black Prince who, in 1355, indulged himself in putting to the sack and wiping out the unfortified lower town. The struggles between Armagnacs and Bourguignons, which divided the population, left no trace in the defence system.

The interminable struggle which, throughout their reigns, was taking place along all frontiers of the kingdom between François I (1515-1547) then Henry II (1547-1559) and Charles V and Philip II hardly extended to the Pyrenees frontier except on the west, during Lesparre's campaign into Navarre (1520-1521). However, to provide against every eventuality, in 1543 Marshal Montpezat had the towers and barbicans of the outer southern enceinte fitted up with cannons for flanking, the only remaining trace of the work of this time in Carcassonne's fortifications.

During the wars of Religion, if there was a preoccupation for the security of the stronghold, it is because after having been Viscount Raymond Roger's jail, his castle with deep dungeons was still used as State prison, and there was a dread of a sudden attack by the Huguenots for the deliverance of their coreligionists. Several times — in 1568, 1575, 1585, they unsuccessfully attempted to sack the City. They had connivances inside the stronghold, and above all the support of the lower town which favoured the Protestants. Never, at all events, did the City play a strategic role in the foremost plan in these scattered struggles.

In the following century the importance of the City further diminished; the treaty of the Pyrenees (1659) put an end to a war which had been waged over the battlefields of the North. One of its clauses : the reunion of Roussillon with France, deprived Carcassonne of the importance as a frontier post which it had held until then.

The XVIIth, then XVIIIth centuries were to take away from the City its administrative and religious sway, by the transfer into the lower town of the Presidial (1656) and of the episcopal seat (1745). Saint-Nazaire was to remain an episcopal seat until 1801, when Saint-Michael of the lower town became a cathedral. Thus, in a half sleep state, did the Revolution find it.

VIOLLET-LE-DUC'S. RESTORATION.

Under the Revolution and during the first half of the XIXth century, the City was no more than an arsenal or barracks, a function which the castle maintained up to within the last few years.

However, the useless ramparts were left without repairs. Moreover, the inhabitants of the environs were allowed freely to use it as a quarry for stone. Thus in 1807 the Treasury tower, one of Philip le Hardi's finest buildings, was given over to the use of the Carcassonne Hospital. The demolition, fortunately, was only partial, but fragments of stone bosses coming from it are still to be seen in the basements of the hospital, on the side washed by the stream of the Aude (1).

Public opinion was roused by such conduct, and this sale was stopped by authority. In 1835, Mérimée published his Notes on Travels in the Midi of France, drawing attention to the City. From 1844, Viollet-le-Duc had undertaken the restoration of Saint Nazaire cathedral when, in 1850, a decree condemned the whole of the military works to demolition.

Energetic action led by Cros-Mayrevieille resulted in the annulling of the decree. In 1855, Viollet-le-Duc, who since 1844 had undertaken the restoration of Saint-Nazaire, began the restoration of the ramparts, which went on until the end of the century and is not completely finished in our day; some recent military buildings still stand inside the courtyard of the castle.

---

(1) Pierre EMBRY : *Sale of the Tresau Tower, June 22, 1807, in Mem. of the Soc. of Arts and Sciences of Carcassonne,* 3rd series, vol. IV, 1935-1936, p. 235, 242, and separate reprint.

CONSPECTUS OF THE VISIT OF THE CITY

Itinerary	Source and date	Most remarkable characteristics	Observations
THE AUDE BARBICAN (41).	Epoch of Saint Louis between 1240 and 1260.	Formerly an outwork of circular form, destroyed and replaced by the church of Saint Gimer. It was reached by a slope	It was used for the protection of the Aude Gate.
THE AUDE DOORWAY (16).	Same period.	The ascent to the Aude Doorway is steep and strongly defended. The outer gateway is formed by a sunken door followed by another in tierce-point. *Next to it*, The Seneschal Gate, an oblong courtyard, a small door, a staircase leading to the Aude Doorway : a semicircular opening in the Visigothic curtain.	Numerous alterations since the vth century.
	Almost entirely of the second quarter of the xiith century.	THE CASTLE.	
1º Eastern Barbican.	Saint Louis.	Semi-circular.	
2º Exterior-east front.		It is of a geometrical simplicity, encircled by a dry moat. *From left to right* : St Paul's tower (40), the 2 towers of the East Gate (34-35), the tower of the Barracks fortified with hoards (36), the Major's tower (37). The eastern doorway is narrow and low ; its folding-door was stengthened in the middle ages with two portcullis, whose grooves are to be seen, and these were defended, on the outer side by machicolations.	The bridge in front of it is of the xviith century and replaces the original flying-bridge.
- The great courtyard of the castle.		On the rear side of the gateway will be seen the beautiful twin window of the second floor. **Opposite**, the square keep, whose first floor window was altered in the xviith century. On the floor above, twelfth century embrasures were stopped up in the xiiith century.	In this courtyard of honour the viscounts held court at times. Formerly a twin window, it was deprived of its little separating column in the xviith century.

Itinerary	Source and date	Most remarkable characteristics	Observations
3° The interior guard-room.	xiith to xviith cent.	The vast bays were pierced in the course of various alterations.	Only the small windows with an irregular arc surmounting them formerly lighted the room.
The Museum (1)		*Room I :*	
	Gallo-roman	Milestones, including that of Numerien "prince of youth". Sarcophagus from Tournissan. Sculpted heads.	
		Room II :	
	Merovingian and carolingian periods	Sarcophagus from Floure ornamented with Christian symbols : the vine and corn. Antependium of Saint Gimer with interlaced ornaments.	From the cathedral of Saint Nazaire.
	Roman period	Stone slab with hunting and chivalry motif carvings.	From Rennes-le-Château.
		Original capitals from the northern doorway of Saint-Nazaire.	Donated by Viollet-le-Duc.
		Washing bowl from Lagrasse.	
		Cemetery crosses, some of which are thought to be Cathare.	
		Room III, or the keep room :	
	xiith cent.	On the four walls, remains of frescoes depicting battles and chivalric scenes; borders of animals.	Discovered in 1926 by Pierre Embry.
	xvith cent.	The two-sided Calvary from Villanière.	
		Room IV :	
		Recumbent figure of a knight.	From Lagrasse.
	Late xiith century.	Keystones from the vault Saint Louis	From the Jacobins of Carcassonne.
	xivth cent.	Keystones from the vault Saint Louis of France.	From the Seneschal's court of Carcassonne.
	xivth cent.	Keystones from the vault Saints Pierre and Paul	From the Franciscans of Carcassonne.
	xiiith cent.	Keystones from the vault. Easter lamb.	Local origin.
		Keystones from the vault. Rose.	From the city of Carcassonne.
		Keystones from the vault. Angel.	Jacobins of Carcassonne.

(1) The information about this museum was kindly given us by M. Jacques Riche, chief archivist of the Aude region.

Itinerary	Source and date	Most remarkable characteristics	Observations
		Keystones from the vault decorated with a wing.	Jacobins of Carcassonne.
		Keystones from the vault decorated with Christ giving his blessing.	Lasserre-de-Prouille.
		Five flat tombs stood upright.	From the Franciscans and Augustins of Carcassonne.
		A rectangular fountain basin decorated with arcatures and figures	From Saint Nazaire of Carcassonne.
		Standing against the dividing wall between the two rooms : Angel (xivth cent.)	Discovered in the City while work was in progress on the theatre.
		Room V :	
		Divided transversally by the elevated arcades ot the Grassalio house :	
		In the first part of this room :	
	xiiith cent.	40 simple capitals.	From the choir of Saint Nazaire of Carcassonne.
	xivth cent.	Double capitals of marble.	From the Jacobins of Carcassonne.
	xivth cent.	Statue of a bishop.	From the Jacobins of Carcassonne.
	xivth cent.	Group of the Trinity.	From Nébias.
	xivth cent.	Statue of Saint Basilica.	From Pomas.
		In the second part :	
	xvth cent.	Octagonal font. Statue of the virgin and child.	From the convent of Charity of Carcassonne
		Crows with human heads in a frieze or separately from Saint-Nazaire.	Donated by Viollet-le-duc
		Front of a tomb with figures under arcatures (perhaps Giraud du Puy's), crucifixion	From Caunes
		Room VI :	
		wall basin for the holy oils. Saint André	
		Fragment of capital and crows with human faces. In the window embrasure, china tiles.	From digs in the castle

Itinerary	Source and date	Most remarkable characteristics	Observations
	xvith cent.	In a glass case on the wall, alabaster panels from an altar-piece and two virgins' heads	Fom the church of Saint-Sernin of the city
	xviith cent.	*Room VII.* Carved armorial bearings. This room is reserved for temporary exhibitions concerning Carcassonne. *On the upper floor of the main body of the entrance building.* Model of the ramparts of the City acquired from a private owner. This room will serve as the point of departure for lecture-tours.	
The mosaic.	Ascribed to the iiird century.	Mosaics paving three rooms of a Roman villa have been brought to light.	Discovered in 1923 two metres deep in the courtyard.
The tower of he castle. o Eastern gateway (34-35).	2nd quarter of the xiith c.	The most interesting part of it is a room on the 2nd floor taking up the two towers and the main building which connects them.	Commanded the exterior portcullis of the gateway; one can still see the grooves, augmented on the outside by a machicolation.
o Small ourtyard of he castle.	2nd quarter of the xiith c.	The circuit of this courtyard is made by the round-way which overlooks it. View of Saint Paul's tower (40) in the S. E. The way crosses the Pinte tower (13) all divided into stories which were reached by ladders. Served as watch-tower for the castle.	Notice the fine twin Romanesque window lighting the storey above that of the round-way.
e The Dwelling.	2nd quarter of the xiith c.	Small main building connecting the Pinte tower to the keep. From the windows, curious view downward on to Saint-Gimer.	The indented gable was created arbitrarily by Viollet-le-Duc on the model which the tower of the Treasury offered him.
o The Donon-keep.	2nd quarter of the xiith c. and xiiith c.	Opening directly on to the round-way, this lofty chamber, with simple crenelated flat roof, in xiith c., was recovered in xiiith c.	The pattern of the battlements is repeated in the joints of the stones.

I

Itinerary	Source and date	Most remarkable characteristics	Observations
5º The great court of the castle (by the round-way).	2nd quarter of the XIIth c.	The round-way bends and crosses in particular the Powder tower (39) the chapel tower (12) whose lower storey constituted one of the apses of the chapel.	No communication between the castle and the enceinte of the City. By means of works called traverses or guardwalls, which bestride the lists, this round-way which dominates the inner enceinte commands the paths, in particular the fortified way rising from the Aude barbican.
6º The Staircase Tower. 7º The Major's Tower.	2nd quarter of the XIIth c.	The finest in the castle. Two lower rooms vaulted with fine cupolas. The upper room covers the whole area of the tower. The curtain which comes next was fortified with wooden hoards, restored by Viollet-le-Duc.	An admirable watch-tower. Its eight loopholes are open broadly to every point on the horizon They formed an outer gallery like a balcony, pierced with embrasures which was reached via the opening of the crenellations. Their floor was pierced with machicolations. They were only set up in time of war.
8º The Tower of the Barracks.	Same period.	Also fortified with hoards Notice the fine XIIth century window and the sculptured capital representing Daniel in the lions' den.	
A) *The Tower of Justice* (15).	3rd quarter of the XIIIth c. end of Saint Louis' reign.	THE ENCEINTE FROM THE CASTLE (14) TO THE NARBONNAISE ARCHWAY (1). One of the most beautiful. On the first floor the room of state, where the tribunal sat; it has a pointed-arch vault. On leaving the tower of Justice follow the round-way covered for	Was built in the place of a Visi gothic tower. Viollet-le-Duc reconstructed the crenellation

Itinerary	Source and date	Most remarkable characteristics	Observations
		some way and lit by three fine twin windows of the XIIth c. It continues in the open air.	after two styles; that of the end of the XIIth c. for the first merlons, the Visigothic for the last.
		Perpendicular to it, the traverse of the Seneschal bestrides the lists by way of a defile in a broken curve, constructed in the XVIth century, arbitrarily reconstructed by Viollet-le-Duc in the style of the XIIIth century.	
3) *From the Gateway of the Seneschal to the Bishop's Round Tower.* Outer enceinte : small Canisou tower (51)	Between 1240 and 1260.		Commands the unfortified part of the Aude heights
Inner enceinte Visigothic tower (17).		Horse-shoe plan. A floor formerly separated the two rooms. The base of the tower is solid masonry.	The upper part was rearranged by Viollet-le-Duc.
The curtain.	Vth and end of the XIIIth c.	Restored by Viollet-le-Duc in Vth c. style, by the side of the Visigothic tower, in that of the end of the XIIIth c., near the Bishop's tower.	
The Round Tower (18).	About 1280.	Work covering an extensive sector of the inner enclosure built under Ph. le Hardi, enveloping the S. E. corner of the City and built with particular care. This tower took the place of a Visigothic tower in 1280 and was then granted to the bishop.	Wrongly named after the Inquisition : this tribunal sat in the tower of Justice. It was the episcopal prison. The chains of the basement-room, the scratchings on the walls by the prisoners bear witness to this
The Bishop's Square tower (19).	4th quarter of the XIIIth c.	Overlapping the lists it forms part of the inner and outer curtain-walls, whence its square plan. Its corners are furnished with watch-towers resting on double buttresses which strengthen each angle. The round-way passes round it, leaving it isolated like a redoubt.	Played the part of a lock interrupting movement on the rampart circuit, whence its importance in the defence system.

Itinerary	Source and date	Most remarkable characteristics	Observations
C) *From the Bishop's Square Tower to the south-west angle.* - Outer enceinte : the great Canissou tower (52).	Between 1240 and 1260.	Standard model for the towers of this enceinte — solid and simple on two stories.	Simple purpose of flanking.
- Inner enceinte Cahuzac's tower (20).	4th quarter of the XIIIth c.	Circular plan. Covers under its range the great Canissou tower.	Between Cahuzac's tower and the great Canissou tower the lists are no more than a narrow passage
D) *South-west angle.*		Due to the levelling of the lists the Visigothic buildings, weakened by the loosening of their foundations, have inclined forward. On the other hand, Ph. le Hardi's towers, being very well built, act as stalwart bastions.	The fortifications serve as retaining walls.
- Outer enceinte Burlas (53).	Between 1240 and 1260.	Situated at the extremity of the stronghold's salient; it is an important three-storey work. The remains of an overthrown Visigothic tower discovered in the course of excavations between the two curtain-walls prove that the original Visigothic enceinte coincided, in this sector uniformly, with the present inner enclosure, contrary to what had been believed previously. It also leads us to believe that the Visigothic enceinte was accidentally destroyed.	An undoubtedly erroneous tradition attributed to the top room wide open on the lists the function of grand-stand at the time of the tourneys which would have taken place in the part adjoining the lists Actually it permitted the riddling with arrows of enemies who had managed to instal themselves there.
- Inner enceinte : Mipadre tower (21).	3rd quarter of the XIIIth c.	Situated at the apex of a virtual right angle, furnished with a spire. The round-way bends round it without crossing it, isolating it like a dungeon or keep. It is reached by a spiral staircase of four flights. In the top room, whose floor is missing, will be noticed a fire-place and an oven, enabling the occupants to subsist in case of siege.	

Itinerary	Source and date	Most remarkable characteristics	Observations
E) *From the South - West angle to Saint Martin's tower.* - Outer enceinte : Our-liac Tower (54).	Between 1240 and 1260.	Nearly rectilinear. In the xvith c. a loophole was contrived to harbour a piece of ordnance for flanking.	
Cremade Barbican (55).	Same period.	Vast semi-circular work 15 m. in diameter.	Defends the approach to the du Razès postern.
- Inner enceinte : the South Mill Tower (22).	About 1287.	Fine rostriform tower. A spiral staircase leads to the five rooms placed one above the other in the tower. The recessed round-way goes round the upper storey.	Formerly, on the upper floor, there was a mill; traces of it have disappeared. It served to feed the ovens of the nearby towers and assured their independence. On the town side an open-air theatre has been built whose stage is set up at the foot of the tower.
Saint Nazaire Tower (23).	About 1287.	Built on a square plan; pierced at its base by a passage bent at a right angle constituting the Saint Nazaire postern. Below, in a narrow passage, the embrasures of two loopholes are seen; they surround on the lists the mouth of a well prepared in the masonry and which a folding-door used to close. A spiral staircase ascends to the first floor into a square chamber serving as a guard-room, from which the external portcullis was operated. - On the same floor, external platform from which the portcullis on the City side was worked. The second floor room is very curious; it is covered with a fine vault of ribbed vaulting, very acutely pointed, whose soffits spring from the very ground of the room.	Thanks to the well, at which one could draw from the first floor, to the oven and to the fireplace, the defenders could prolong resistance. The top of the tower, in virtue of its dominant position, was used as a lookout post ,now for the orientation table.

Itinerary	Source and date	Most remarkable characteristics	Observations
Saint Martin's Tower (24).	4th quarter of the XIIIth c.	Rostriform tower. The round-way skirts it without crossing it; it is like a keep. Inside, two low vaulted rooms, a fireplace enabled the third room to be warmed.	
F) *From Saint Martin's tower to Plo tower.* - Outer enceinte : Cautiere (57). tower and Pouletot tower (58).	Between 1240 and 1260.	Built on the plan of the d'Ourliac tower. In front of these towers starts the moat which surrounds the outer enceinte to the East and North.	
- Inner enceinte. (25) Tower of the Prisons. (26) Castéra Tower. (27) Plo Tower.	Vth century to end of the XIIth century.	We again meet the Visigothic enceinte which has been done up by the centuries which followed. This original enceinte having been laid bare at the time of the levelling of the lists, the base was re-made in the XIIth c. The top parts are also of this epoch. Surrounded by this double masonry of the end of the XIIth century appears the vth century construction. Usual vth c. plan, horse-shoe shape. The Castéra tower is slightly leaning, like the Visigothic tower, (cf. p. 15).	Notice the writings scratched on the walls of the rooms in the tower of the Prisons recalling its use as royal prison.
G) *From Balthazar tower (28) to the Narbonnaise Archway* (1). - Outer enceinte : The Vade Tower (60).	1240-1245.	The finest in the outer enceinte. Formerly isolated between the inner enceinte and the outer enceinte of 1228-1239. The latter formed a wide projection, the "truss" of Saint-Michael's mount. The construction, between 1256 and 1260 of the outer enceinte within range of the inner enceinte incorporated the Vade Tower. Served to provide	It owes its name to this function : bada, in Languedoc, means « to gaze ». It might be compared with the contemporary tower of Constance of Aigues-Mortes, at first isolated,

Itinerary	Source and date	Most remarkable characteristics	Observations
		a view beyond the hill of Saint Michael's mount, the only point on the City's approaches which dominates this one. Of five stories, exactly circular. Planned like a keep, a ladder gave access to the first floor. It contains a well, a fireplace and an oven.	and afterwards joined to the enceinte.
Peyre tower (61).	1255-1260.	A strong work, circular, on three floors.	Function of flanking; it had moreover to protect the outlet of an open postern in the curtain which adjoins to the North.
- Inner enceinte : Balthazar Tower (28).	4th quarter of the XIIIth c.	The only one in this vast S. E. front to preserve no Vth century remains. Equipped with a watch tower.	
Davejean Tower (29). Saint Laurent Tower (30). Trouquet Tower (31). Saint-Sernin Sacrarium Tower (32).	Vth century and 4th quarter of the XIIIth c.	Of Visigothic origin Also superpositions of masonry of the Vth and XIIIth centuries. The tower of the Saint Sernin Sacrarium presents a fine Gothic window with flamboyant tracery, dating from 1441	It served as apse to the chapel of the original castle, and after the abandonment of the latter in the XIIth century was used anew as apse for Saint Sernin church built in the XIIth century and destroyed at the Revolution.
A) *Series* : *Narbonnaise Archway* (1 & 2) *and Treasure tower* (3). - Outer enceinte : Narbonnaise outer archway.	XIXth c. Boeswillwald. (successor to Viollet-le-Duc in 1880).	FROM THE NARBONNAISE ARCHWAY TO THE CHARPENTIERE TOWER. Unity of the Bridge crossing the moat and of the small crenellated castle set above an arcade which	Somewhat fanciful restoration.

Itinerary	Source and date	Most remarkable characteristics	Observations
		surrounds it. Notice in front the statue of Dame Carcas, legendary heroine of the city. (XVIth c.)	
Saint Louis Barbican. (43)	Between 1240 and 1260.	By a semi-circular door pierced at the side of the Saint Louis Barbican, (43), the lists are entered.	
Bérard tower (44).	About 1260.	Marks the extremity of the nearly rectilinear part of the east front.	
- Inner enceinte : The Narbonnaise archway (1 and 2).	End of the XIIIth c.	With the Treasure tower, constitutes the most perfect ensemble of the epoch. Formed of two twin towers, united by a main building and encompassing the thoroughfare to the Gate. Between the towers 25 m. high, not counting roofing, 10 m. wide, 15 deep, runs a small passage 8 ft. wide defended at the entrance and exit by a machicolated portcullis. In a niche surrounded by three angel figures, a XIVth century statue of the Virgin. The Child whom she held on her left arm has disappeared. The interior arrangements are planned like those of a keep equipped with the resources necessary for prolonging resistance when isolated. The only room on the second storey, covering the area of both the towers, is the vastest and finest in the City; it is lit on the town side by five elegant windows.	So called because it is open to the E. towards Narbonne. On the ground floor, loopholes enabled the garrison to watch comings and goings.
Treasure tower. (3)	4th quarter of the XIIIth c.	Its name comes from its application from the beginning of the use of the royal Treasury. The round-way bends round it on the outside, along its flat front facing the town. Its gable is flanked by high watch-towers.	Also served, later, as a prison, as testify the traces of bar fastenings dotting several windows.
B) *The North Front.* - Outer enceinte : Benazet tower (45).	1240 to 1260.	Regular polygonal outline almost inscribed in a semi-circle. All cut the round-way, and are two-storey, except the Moreti tower.	

Itinerary	Source and date	Most remarkable characteristics	Observations
Notre-Dame Barbican (46) Moreti Tower (47). Glacière Tower (48). Porte rouge Tower (49). West watch-tower (50).			
Inner enceinte: Constable's Mill Tower (4).	vth and xiiith century.	Series of six Visigothic towers. Its dominant position made it be chosen as wind-mill. The flour poured away into sacks through the two ducts which come out at the foot of the adjoining curtain.	Still the same superposition of styles.
Vieulas Tower (5).		One of the most ruined of the enceinte, which sank in part at the time of the levelling of the lists.	Its fall had repercussions on the neighbouring curtains.
Marquière Tower (6).	vth and xiiith century.	Tower leaning toward the East; two-storey. The lower floor windows are Visigothic and the side windows, blocked up in the xiiith century, have been converted into loop-holes.	Commands, in the outer enceinte, Notre-Dame Barbican. Cuts the round-way and obliges those who are following it to descend one storey by a ladder.
Samson Tower (8).	vth century.	The cube base is of the vth century; the remainder was rebuilt in the xixth century. Viollet-le-Duc's restoration is not invariably in excellent style; it over-multiplied the brick cordons.	
Avar Mill Tower (9).	vth century.	Same characteristics.	Traces of the mill have disappeared in the course of restoration.
Charpentière Tower (11).	vth century.	Also Visigothic, restored in this style by Viollet-le-Duc. Only the solid core at the centre is authentic Visigothic.	A branch of the workshops where the wooden works were prepared. Whence its name.

Itinerary	Source and date	Most remarkable characteristics	Observations
		SAINT-NAZAIRE'S CATHEDRAL	
	End of the xith century to beginning of the xivth c.		Only became a cathedral at the beginning of the xth c., when bishop Saint Gimer abandoned the town and Saint Mary's cathedral to take refuge in the City. Nothing remains of the first cathedral, not even the crypt as it has sometimes been asserted.
Exterior.		Very much restored by Viollet-le-Duc who remade nearly all the sculpture on it. Fortified. The west façade, for reasons of defence, possesses no door, and its gable is surmounted by a watch gallery.	
	Romanesque.	To the North, main entrance. The barrel-shaped archings spring from five small columns ornamented with capitals. An octogonal tower at the north-west corner of the transept. At its foot opens a Gothic doorway surmounted by a beautiful rose window of the end of the xiiith c.	Only the two capitals near the door are original. The others, like the spandrel, the pier, the modillions of the cornice are the work of Viollet-le-Duc.
	Gothic.	The chevet, polygonal, typical of the Gothic architecture of the South of France. The shoring up is done directly by buttresses without the medium of flying buttresses. It is lit by long windows with two lancets divided by a mullion. The east wall of the transept, by windows with three lancets.	
	Gothic.	In front of the south facade, Radulphe's chapel, prolonged westwards by a sacristy. A low and simple edifice. The choir is composed of a polygonal apse and a straight bay and the nave has two straight bays.	
Interior		Entrance is by the Romanesque north doorway. One is struck by the contrast between two very distinct parts.	

Itinerary	Source and date	Most remarkable characteristics	Observations
	Finished in the 1st half of the XIIth c.	1° THE NAVE is Romanesque, very sombre. Is composed of six bays. The great arches and arch-bands of the vault in ribbed-vaulting spring alternately from square pillars flanked with four attached half-columns and from thick round pillars. The aisles, very narrow, are covered by a semi-circular vault whose soffits spring from the level of those of the nave vault. Nave and aisles have a common roof : with two slopes, very simple. The half-columns flanking the square pillars rear up their capitals more or less high according as they take the springings from the great arches or from the binding-joints; on the other hand, the round pillars have only one capital, fine round cluster of two courses. Notice the Romanesque holy-water basin in the 4th bay to the north of the nave. In the south aisle a walled-up doorway formerly leading to the Romanesque cloister. It is adorned with a fragment of a Romanesque sarcophagus. In the XVth and XVIth c. there were built between two western bays of the aisle two chapels, one dedicated to Joan of Arc, the other occupied by baptismal fonts.	An arrangement which admits light only by means of narrow windows pierced in the walls of the side-aisles, and by the small open eyes in the west wall. Decoration of the capitals varied : motifs derived from the waterleaf, the Corinthian capital, the Carolingian interlaced ornaments or geometrical motifs. The organs and their loft are of the XVIIth cent. Behind this basin a deep niche in the wall of the aisle is the only remnant of the ancient chapel of St Andrew (XVIth c.) done away by with Viollet-le Duc
	Built about 1269 on the site of the Romanesque transept and choir. The vaults were completed under Bishop Peter de Rochefort (1300-1322).	2° THE TRANSEPT AND THE CHOIR are both excellent Gothic. Each arm of the transept consists of three rectangular bays, and on the smallest side of each bay to the East opens a small chapel consisting of two bays. The arches separating the two bays of each chapel, and the chapels between them are long, light and elegant. The upper part of the north wall is lit by a fine circular rose. The upper part of the south wall	In the design of the pillars and capitals is manifest the wish - uncommon at that time - to harmonise the Gothic ornament with that of the Romanesque nave which was preserved. This window-tracery, later than

I

Itinerary	Source and date	Most remarkable characteristics	Observations
		looks like a vast glass case because the rose is framed in a bent curve with angles in open work. The *choir*, formed by a straight bay and a polygonal apse.	the north window tracery, is o xivth century. The straight ba is covered by sexpartite vault exceptional at the end of the xiiith c
	xvith c. xvth c. beginning of the xivth c.	The *statuary* of choir and transept is abundant. *One finds :* Polychromatic Pieta, against the north wall of the transept, a tomb of a bishop, perhaps Geraud du Puy, against the sanctuary columns, 22 New Testament personages. These are, starting from the first pillar on the left-hand side of the altar : 1. The Virgin 2. St Joachim 3. St Celsus 4. St Nazaire 5. St Anne 6. The Angel Gabriel 7. St Bartholomew 8 to 17. Ten other apostles 18. St Helena carrying the true Cross 19. The twelfth apostle 20. St Gimer, bishop and founder of the church. 21. Christ 22. The angel of the Passion.	
		THE STAINED glass windows are remarkable. - *N. Rose :* general tonality green and violet. In the centre, Virgin attended by angel thurifers. In the trefoils at the point of the twelve petals of the rose, Virgins and Confessors; and, in those of the circumference, angels. - *S. Rose :* warmer tonality. In the centre Christ in Majesty accompanied with the armorial bearings of bishop Peter de Rochefort. In the trefoils and quatrefoils, animals symbolical of the four evangelists and effigies of Church Fathers and ancient philosophers.	See them preferably in the morning or in the early afternoon.

Itinerary	Source and date	Most remarkable characteristics	Observations
	xivth c.	- The stained-glass windows of the side chapels correspond. *To the left* (north) an illustration of a scholastic treatise by Saint Bonaventure entitled "Dignum vitæ"; tree of Jesse; in the trefoils of the upper part the Last Judgement is portrayed : in the trefoils of the sides, the Resurrection of the dead. The right window shows in its lower part Adam and Eve surrounded by Noah's ark and the ark of the covenant substituted, in the xixth c. for the picture of the four rivers of Paradise. To events from the Life of Christ are united twelve virtues, and personages from the Old Testament. A text from Saint Bonaventura is inscribed on a scroll along the framework.	Its interpretation is more obscure and has only recently been given by Canon J. Gals.
	Beginning of the xivth c.	- In the *choir*, five stained-glass windows, three of which are legendary, formed of small medallions superposed. *That to the N.* represents *on the left* the lives of Saint Peter and Saint Paul. *That to the S.* the lives of Saint Nazaire and Saint Celsus. *The centre one*, the Life of Christ.	Read each lancet from bottom to top. Read from left to right going from one lancet to another and starting at the bottom.
	xvith c. connected with the school of Toulouse.	*Those of the intermediate windows* represent patrons of the diocese : Saint Celsus presented to Saint Nazaire by his mother, to the N., and the childhood of the Virgin to the S.	
		THE CHAPELS.	
	xivth c.	At the last bays of the nave, two symmetrical chapels each of two bays :	
	Built during the lifetime of this bishop (1300-1320) only completed after his death to take in his monument.	- *That to the North*, known by the name of Peter de Rochefort's chapel. His tomb-stone is set in the ground a little forward. In three niches surmounted by gables, a fine statue of the bishop, surrounded by those of the two archdeacons Pons de Castillon and Gasc de Rochefort.	Probably rebuilt by Viollet-le-Duc.

Itinerary	Source and date	Most remarkable characteristics	Observations
		Under the basement thirteen clerks and canons form the funeral procession.	
	Same period	*In front*, statues of SS Peter and Paul.	
	Created by Bishop Rodier (1324-1330).	- *that to the South, Peter Rodier's :* held his tomb, long since vanished. A keystone and a stained-glass window still bear the arms of the founder.	
	Ist half of the xiiith c.	Facing the altar, curious bas-relief known by the name of « stone of the siege », representing perhaps the death of Simon de Montfort before Toulouse or the Siege of the City in 1240	
	Anterior to the construction of the choir and transept.	- *Radulphe's Chapel :* separate edifice. Up against the east wall is fixed the tomb of the bishop, surrounded by an architectural border. His effigy stands out in demi-relief in a shallow niche. He is standing and is blessing with his right hand. At his feet is figured the sarcophagus resting on three small columns. The lower part represents the death of the prelate surrounded by his canons.	William Radulphe or better Razouls (1255-1266) had this chapel built. Partially filled up in the xvith c. It was cleared in xixth c.
Interior of the City.		It is interesting to go over the network of lanes which intersect at picturesque crossways. Notice the kerbs of medieval wells in two small squares, the rue de la Paix, whose houses are leaning against the inside of the ramparts, the statue of our Lady of travellers (XVth c.) at the corner of rue du Piô and rue Cros-Mayrevielle.	

The illustrations in this book are by courtesy of M. Henri Paillasson, Grenoble, with the exception of : N⁰ 2 (Perceval, Paris) ; Nᵒˢ 35, 43, 53 (Antoine Trincano, Lyon) ; N⁰ 54 (Yan, Toulouse). Plates exclusive to Arthaud, photographers : Henri Paillasson and Antoine Trincano.

A SHORT BIBLIOGRAPHY.

The key work on the City of Carcassonne is constituted by the following important books :

Joseph Poux, Archivist of the department of the Aude : *The City of Carcassonne, history and description*. Drawings and cuts by Pierre Embry.

1st vol. : « *The origins up to the accession of the Counts of the House of Barcelona* (1067), in-4, 2nd ed. Toulouse, 1931.

2nd vol. : *The Growth* (1067-1466), 2 vol. in-4, Toulouse and Paris, 1931.

3rd vol. : *The Decline*. — *The Restoration* (1466-1937), 2 vol. in-4, Toulouse and Paris, 1938.

An abridgment was given :

Joseph Poux : *The City of Carcassonne. An Historical, archaelogical and descriptive summary*. 1 vol. in-8. Toulouse, 1925.

It will be profitable to consult the following books that are easily read :

P. Foncin : *An historical, archaelogical and descriptive Guide of the City of Carcassonne*, in-8, Carcassonne, 1866.

Gaston Jourdanne : *Carcassonne*, in-8, Carcassonne, 1900.

Louis Fédié : *History of Carcassonne, lower town and City*, in-8, Carcassonne, s. d.

E. Viollet-le-Duc : *City of Carcassonne (Aude)*. Paris, 1858, in-8.

———

1. Southern façade of the City

2. Aerial wiew of the City
(next page)

4. **Les tours des Casernes et du Major (château)**
   The Barracks Tower and the Major's Tower (castle)
   Kasernenturm und Major-Turm (Schloß)
   Torre delle Caserme e Torre del Major (Castello)
   Torre de los Cuarteles y del Mayor (castillo)

3. **La Porte d'Aude**
   The Aude Gate
   Das Aude-Tor
   Porta d'Aude
   Puerta del Aude

5. **La Cité vue des bords de l'Aude**
   The City from the banks of the Aude
   Die Altstadt, vom Aude-Ufer aus
   La Cité vista dalle rive dell'Aude
   La Cité, vista desde las orillas del Aude

6

6.

Courtines entre la to
  des Casernes et
  tour du Major
Curtains between th
  Barracks Tower a
  the Major's Tower
Die hölzernen Ku
  tinen zwische
  Kasernen-und Majo
  Turm
Cortine fra la torr
  delle Caserme e
  torre del Major
Cortinas entre la tor
  de los Cuarteles
  la del Mayor

7.

La tour des Caserne
  vue de la grand
  cour du château
The Barracks Towe
  seen from the grea
  courtyard of th
  castle
Der Kasernenturr
  vom Großen Schlo
  hof
La torre delle Ca
  erme vista dall
  grande corte de
  castello
La torre de los Cuar
  teles vista desde e
  patio principal de
  Castillo

8.

Tour de Justice, tou
  Pinte et tour de
  Poudre
The Justice Tower, th
  Pinte Tower and th
  Powder Tower
Justizturm, Pinteturr
  und Pulverturm
Torre di Giustizi
  torre Pinte e torr
  della Polvere
Torre de la Justici
  torre Pinte y torr
  de la Pólvora

9. Tours de la Porte orientale et tour Saint-Paul
   Towers of the Eastern Gate and Saint-Paul's Tower
   Die Türme der Ostpforte und der St-Paul-Turm
   Torri della Porta orientale e torre di San Paolo
   Torres de la Puerta Oriental y de San Pablo

10. Porte de la Barbacane
    The Barbican Gate
    Die Barbakane-Pforte
    Porta della Barbacane
    Puerta de la Barbacana

11. **Sarcophage de Floure**
    Sarcophagus from Floure
    Sarkophag von Floure
    Sarcofago di Floure
    Sarcófago de Floure

12. **Cuve à ablutions de Lagrasse**
    Washing bowl from Lagrasse
    Waschbecken aus Lagrasse
    Tinozza per abluzioni di Lagrasse
    Pila de abluciones de Lagrasse

13. **Croix de cimetière, dont certaines présumées cathares**
    Cemetary crosses, some of which are thought to be cathare
    Friedhofskreuze, von denen einige vermutlich von Katharern
       stammen
    Croci di cimitero, alcune delle quali ritenute catare
    Cruces de cementerio, supuestas algunas de ellas cátaras

13

14

14-15-16. Calvaire de Villanière. Détail de sculp-
ture, les deux faces du
calvaire
Calvary from Villanière.
Detail of the sculpture,
the calvary : front and
back
Kalvarienberg von Villa-
nière. Skulpturteil,
Vorder-und Rückseite
Calvario di Villanière.
Particolare della scul-
tura, insieme delle due
faccie del Calvario
Calvario de Villanière.
Pormenor de escultura,
conjunto de cada una
de sus dos caras

16

17. Devant de tombeau à personnages
Front of the tomb with figures
Detail einer Grabplatte mit Personendarstellungen
Parte anteriore di tomba con personaggi
Frente de un sepulcro con personajes

18. Arcades de la maison Grassalio
Arcades of the Grassalio house
Die Arkaden des Hauses Grassalio
Arcate della casa Grassalio
Arcadas de la mansión de Grassalio

19. Vierge et Enfant
    Virgin and Child
    Heilige Jungfrau mit Kind
    Vergine col Bambino
    Virgen con el Niño

20. Fenêtre romane du château
    A roman window in the castle
    Romanisches Fenster
    Finestra romanica del castello
    Ventana románica del Castillo

21. L'église Saint-Gimer et la ville actuelle vues depuis cette fenêtre
Saint Gimer's Church and today's town seen from this window
Aussicht aus diesem Fenster : die Saint-Gimer Kirche und die
moderne Stadt
Chiesa di San Gimer e la città attuale viste dalla suddetta finestra
La iglesia de San Gimer y la ciudad moderna vistas desde esta
misma ventana

22. Les tours de Cahuzac et du Grand Canissou
The Cahuzac Tower and the Big Canissou Tower
Der Cahuzac - und der Großen Canissou - Turm
Torri di Cahuzac e del Gran Canissou
Las torres de Cahuzac y del Gran Canissou

23. La tour Mipadre
The Mipadre Tower
Der Mipadre-Turm
Torre Mipadre
La torre Mipadre

22

23

24. La tour carrée de l'Evêque — The Bishop's Square Tower — Der quadratische Bischofsturm — Torre quadrata del Vescovo — Torre cuadrada del Obispo

24

25. La tour Wisigothe et les tours ronde et carrée de l'Evêque
The Visigothic Tower and the Bishop's Round and Square Towers
Der westgotische Turm, der runde und der quadratische Bischofsturm
Torre Visigota e torri rotonda e quadrata del Vescovo
La torre visigótica y las torres redonda y cuadrada del Obispo

26. Fossé, barbacane Saint-Louis et avant-porte Narbonnaise
The moat, the Saint Louis Barbican and the Narbonne Gateway
Graben, Saint-Louis Barbakane und Narbonnaise-Vorpforte
Fossato, Barbacane San Luigi e avanporta Narbonese
Foso, barbacana de San Luís y antepuerta Narbonese

28

27. **Tour Saint-Nazaire — The Saint Nazaire Tower — Saint-Nazaire Turm — Torre San Nazaro — Torre de San Nazario**

28. **Tour d'Ourliac, au fond tour du Grand Burlas**
   The Ourliac Tower with the Big Burlas Tower in the background
   Ourliac-Turm, im Hintergrund Grand-Burlas-Turm
   Torre d'Ourliac, sullo sfondo torre del Gran Burlas
   Torre del Ourliac, en el fondo torre del Gran Burlas

29. **De gauche à droite : tours d'Ourliac, du Moulin du Midi et de Mipadre**
   From left to right : The Ourliac, South Mill and Mipadre Towers
   Von links nach rechts : Ourliac, Moulin du Midi-und Mipadre-Turm
   Da sinistra a destra : torri d'Ourliac, del Mulino di Mezzogiorno e Mipadre
   De izquierda a derecha : torres del Ourliac, del Molino del Sur y de Mipadre

30. Tours du Tréseau et de Bérard
   The Tréseau and Bérard Towers
   Tréseau-und Bérard-Turm
   Torre del Tréseau e torre Bérard
   Torres del Tréseau y de Bérard

31. Les lices
   The lists
   Die Turnierplätze
   Le lizze
   Las lizas

32. Avant-porte et porte Narbonnaise — The Narbonne Gateway and Gate — Narbonnaise-Vorpforte und Pforte — Avanporta e porta Narbonese — Antepuerta y Puerta Narbonense

30

33

33. Avant-porte Narbonnaise et buste de Dame Carcas (XVIᵉ siècle).
A cette statue est rattachée la légende du siège de Carcassonne sous Charlemagne : Dame Carcas défendant la Cité et sonnant les cloches pour appeler Charlemagne; « Carcas sonne! » criaient les soldats.

The Narbonne Gateway and bust of Dame Carcas (16th Century).
This statue recalls the legendary siege of Carcassonne in the time of Charlemagne when Dame Carcas defended the City and rang the bells to call Charlemagne. "Carcas is ringing!" (Fr. "Carcas sonne!") cried the soldiers

Narbonnaise-Vorpforte und Statue der "Dame Carcas". Eine beherzte Frau, Dame Carcas, läutete während der Belagerung von Carcassonne die Glocken, um Karl den Großen herbeizurufen. Da riefen die Soldaten : "Carcas sonne!", d.h. Frau Carcas läutet.

Avanporta Narbonese e busto della Dama Carcas (XVIᵉ sec.).
A questa statua è legata la leggenda dell'assedio di Carcassona sotto Carlomagno : la Dama Carcas che difende la città e suona le campane per chiamare Carlomagno. "Carcas suona!" gridavano i soldati.

Antepuerta Narbonense y busto de Dama Carcas (Siglo XVI).
Se aplica a esta figura la leyenda del sitio de Carcasona bajo Carlomagno : Dama Carcas defendiendo la ciudad y tocando las campanas a rebato para llamar a Carlomagno : "Carcas suena" gritaban los soldados.

34

34. Vue plongeante sur l'avant-porte
    Looking down on to the Gateway
    Tiefblick auf die Vorpforte
    Vista dall'alto sull'avanporta
    Vista desde lo alto a la antepuerta

35. La porte Narbonnaise
    The Narbonne Gate
    Narbonnaise-Pforte
    Porta Narbonese
    La puerta Narbonense

36. La Cité vue de la salle du second étage
The City seen from the second floor chamber
Die Altstadt vom Saal des zweiten Stockes aus
La città vista dalla sala del secondo piano
La Cité desde la sala de la segunda planta

37. Cheminée de la salle des gardes
The Guardroom fireplace
Kamin im Wachensaal
Camino della sale delle guardie
Chimenea de la sala de Guardias

37

38. Les lices ; à droite, tours du Sacraire
    Saint-Sernin et du Trauquet ; en
    arrière, à gauche, tour de Balthazar,
    tours de la Peyre et de la Vade
The lists : on the right the Sacraire
    Saint-Sernin tower and the Trau-
    quet tower. In the background, on
    the left, the Balthazar tower, and
    the Peyre and Vade towers
Die Turnierplätze ; rechts, Sacraire
    Saint-Sernin-Turm und Trauquet-
    Turm ; im Hintergrund links,
    Balthasar - La Peyre - und La
    Vade-Turm
Le Lizze ; a destra : torre del Sacrario
    di San Sernino e del Trauquet. Sullo
    sfondo, a sinistra, torre di Bal-
    thazar, torre della Peyre e torre
    della Vade
Las lizas ; a la derecha : torre del
    Sacrarium de San Sernin y del
    Trauquet ; por detrás a la iz-
    quierda : torre Baltasar, torres de
    la Peyre y de la Vade

38

39. Barbacane Notre-Dame. Au fond, tours de Samson et du Moulin d'Avar
   The Notre-Dame Barbican. In the background, the Samson and Avar
   Mill Towers
   Die Notre-Dame Barbakane. In Hintergrund, Samson-Turm und Moulin
   d'Avar-Turm
   Barbacane Notre Dame. Sullo sfondo, torri di Sansone e del Mulino d'Avar
   Barbacana de Nª Sª. En el fondo, torres de Sansón y del Molino de Avar

40. Tours du Vieulas et du Moulin du Connétable (à gauche)
   The Vieulas Tower and the Constable's Mill Tower (left)
   Vieulas-Turm und Moulin du Connétable-Turm (links)
   Torri del Vieulas e del Mulino del Connestabile (a sinistra)
   Torre del Vieulas y del molino del Condestable (a la izquierda)

41. 42. Rosace et croisillon nord (fin XIIIᵉ siècle)
   Rose-window in the north crossbrace (late 13th century)
   Die Rose im Nordquerschiff (Ende XIII . Jh.)
   Rosone della crocera nord (fine del XIII° sec.)
   Rosetón del crucero Norte (fines del siglo XIII)

40

43. **Contreforts**
   Buttresses
   Strebepfeiler
   Contrafforti
   Contrafuertes

44. **Chevet et transept**
   The chevet and the transept
   Chorhaupt und Querschiff
   Abside e transetto
   Presbiterio y crucero

45. Nef et bas-côtés vus du chœur
   (XII⁰ siècle)
   The nave and aisles from the
   choir (12th century)
   Inneres : Schiff und Seitenschiffe
   vom Chor aus (XII . Jh.)
   Navata mediana e navate late-
   rali viste dal coro (XII° sec.)
   La Nave y naves laterales desde
   el coro (S. XII)

46. L'Evêque Radulphe, détail de
   son tombeau
   Bishop Radulphe, a detail of
   his tomb
   Detail vom Grabmal des
   Bischofs Radulphe
   Particolare della tomba del
   Vescovo Radulphe
   El Obispo Radulfo, pormenor
   de su sepulcro

47 et 49. Statues des piliers du chœur
   Pillar statues in the choir
   Statuen von den Chorpfeilern
   Statue dei pilastri del coro
   Estatuas de los pilares del Coro

48. Vitraux du chœur
   Stained-glass windows in the choir
   Glasgemälde aus dem Chor
   Vetrate del Coro
   Vidrieras del Coro

50 et 51. Chapiteaux romans
Roman capitals
Romanische Kapitelle
Capitelli romanici
Capiteles románicos

52. Sculpture du chœur
Sculpture in the choir
Chorskulptur
Scultura del coro
Escultura del Coro

53. Bénitier
Holy water basin
Weihwasserbecken
Acquasantiera
Pila de agua bendita

54. La Cité illuminée
The City lit up
Beleuchtung der Altstadt
La Cité illuminata
La Cité iluminada

54

48 49

TABLE OF ILLUSTRATIONS

Cover. Page 1 : *the two city walls and the western façade of the city of Carcassone near the Count's Castle. The Justice Tower and the south face of the castle from the Seneschal Traverse.*
Page 4 : *stained-glass windows in the choir of the Basilica of Saint-Nazaire.*

1. *Southern façade of the City.*
2. *Aerial view of the City.*
3. *The Aude Gate.*
4. *The Barracks Tower and the Major's Tower (castle).*
5. *The City from the banks of the Aude.*

CASTLE

6. *Curtains between the Barracks Tower ant the Major's Tower.*
7. *The Barracks tower seen from the great courtyard of the castle.*
8. *The Justice Tower, the Pinte Tower and the Powder Tower.*
9. *Towers of the Eastern Gate and Saint Paul's Tower.*
10. *The Barbican Gate.*

LAPIDARY COLLECTION

11. *Floure's sarcophagus.*
12. *Washing-bowl from Lagrasse.*
13. *Cemetery crosses, some of which are thought to be Cathare.*
14-15-16. *Calvary from Villanière. Detail of the sculpture; the calvary : front and back.*
17. *Front of tomb with figures.*
18. *Arcades of the Grassalio house.*
19. *Virgin and Child.*

CASTLE

20. *A roman window in the castle.*
21. *Saint-Gimer's church and today's town seen from this window.*

THE RAMPARTS

22. *The Cahuzac Tower and the Big Canissou Tower from the Bishop's Square Tower.*
22. *The Mipadre Tower with the Cahuzac and Big Canissou Towers in the background.*
24. *The Bishop's Square Tower.*

25. *The Visigothic Tower and the Bishop's Round and Square Towers.*
26. *The moat, the Saint-Louis Barbican and the Narbonne Gateway.*
27. *The Saint-Nazaire Tower.*
28. *The Ourliac Tower with the Big Burlas Tower in the background.*
29. *From left to right : the Ourliac, South Mill and Mipadre Towers.*
30. *The Tréseau and Bérard Towers.*
31. *The lists near the Narbonne Gate.*

THE RAMPARTS : THE NARBONNE GATEWAY AND GATE

32. *The Narbonne Gateway and Gate.*
33. *The Narbonne Gateway and bust of Dame Carcas (16th century). This statue recalls the legendary seige of Carcassonne in the time of Charlemagne when Dame Carcas defended the City and rang the bells to call Charlemagne. " Carcas is ringing ! " (Fr. Carcas sonne !) cried the soldiers.*
34. *Looking down on to the Narbonne Gateway.*
35. *The Narbonne Gate.*
36. *The City seen from the second floor chamber.*
37. *The Guardroom fireplace.*

THE RAMPARTS

38. *The lists : on the right the Sacraire Saint-Sernin Tower and the Trauquet Tower. In the background, on the left, the Balthazar Tower, and the Peyre and Vade Towers.*
39. *The Notre-Dame Barbican. In the background, the Samson and Avar Mill Towers.*
40. *The Vieulas Tower and the Constable's Mill Tower (left).*

SAINT-NAZAIRE'S CATHEDRAL

41. *Rose window in the north crossbrace.*
42. *Interior of the north crossbrace (late 13th century).*
43. *Buttresses.*
44. *The chevet and the transept.*
45. *The nave and aisles from the choir (12th century).*
46. *Bishop Radulphe, a detail of his tomb.*
44-49. *Pillar statues in the choir.*
48. *Stained-glass window in the choir.*
50-51. *Roman capitals.*
52. *Sculpture in the choir.*
53. *Holy water basin.*
54. *The city lit up on the 14th July.*

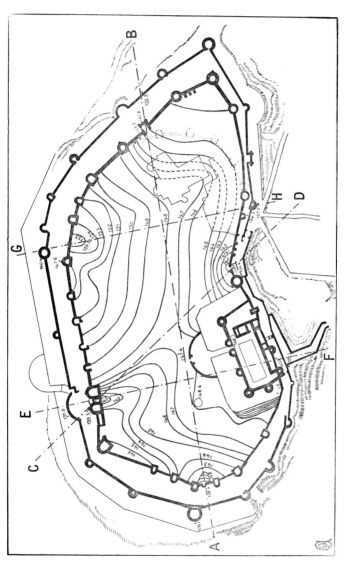

DEVELOPMENT OF THE INNER ENCEINTE AND THE DIFFERENT BUILDING CAMPAIGNS

(Surveys made by Mr. Pierre EMBRY).

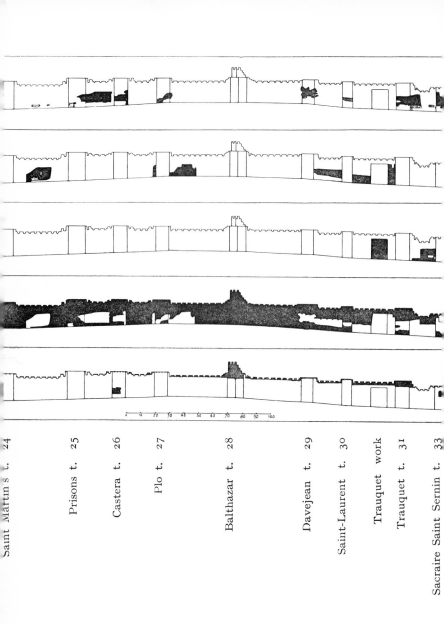

Saint Martin s t. 24

Prisons t. 25

Castera t. 26

Plo t. 27

Balthazar t. 28

Davejean t. 29

Saint-Laurent t. 30

Trauquet work

Trauquet t. 31

Sacraire Saint Sernin t. 33

0 10 20 30 40 50 60 70 80 90 100

A CONTOUR MAP OF TH

(Surveys m

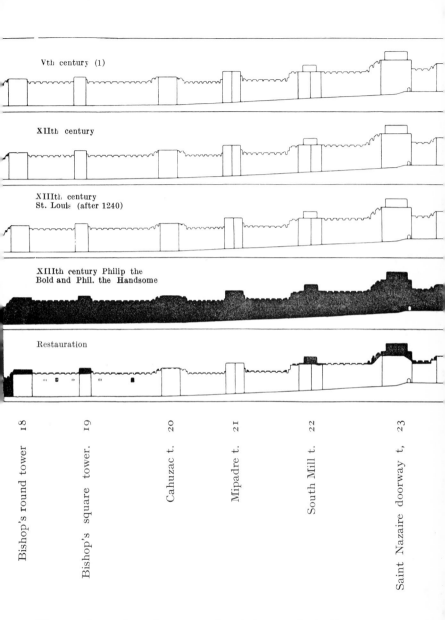

Vth century (1)

XIIth century

XIIIth century
St. Louis (after 1240)

XIIIth century Philip the
Bold and Phil. the Handsome

Restauration

18 Bishop's round tower

19 Bishop's square tower.

20 Cahuzac t.

21 Mipadre t.

22 South Mill t.

23 Saint Nazaire doorway t,

The numbers after the name of each tower refer to the map on p. 95

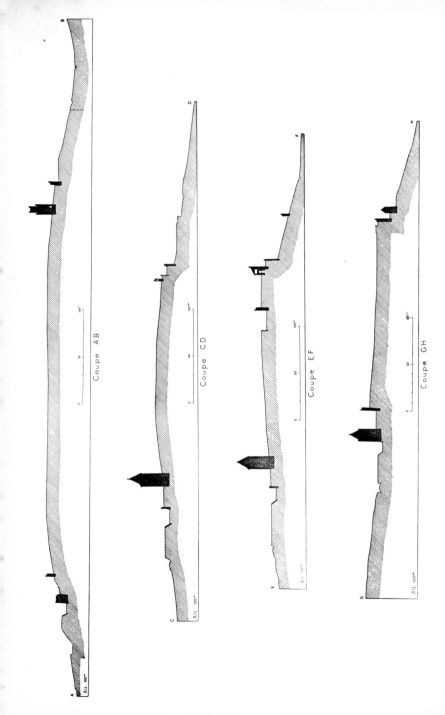

Coupe AB

Coupe CD

Coupe EF

Coupe GH

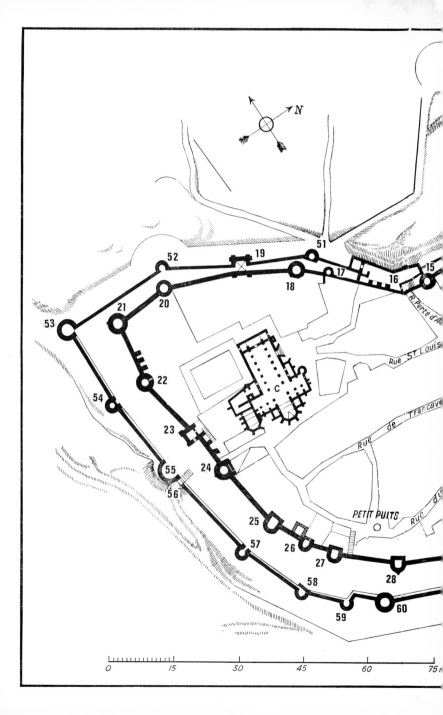

Visigothic t. destroyed

Charpentiere t. 11

Visigothic t. (destroyed) and XIIIth century postern

Chapel t. 12

Powder t. 39

first keep

second keep

Pinte t. 13

Justice t. 15

Aude doorway 16

Visigothic t. 17

Castle

(1) The dotted parts indicate the Visigothic foundations still visi

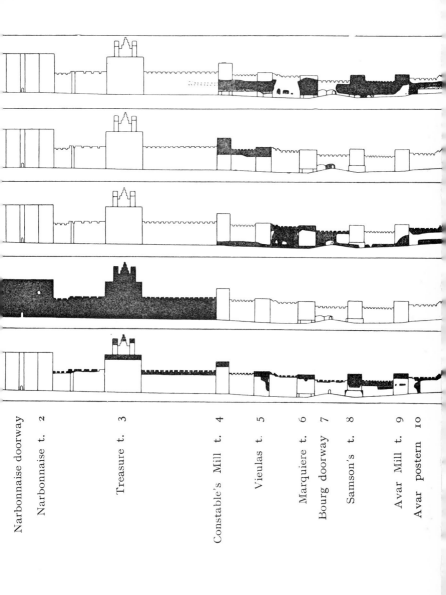

Narbonnaise doorway
Narbonnaise t. 2
Treasure t. 3
Constable's Mill t. 4
Vieulas t. 5
Marquiere t. 6
Bourg doorway 7
Samson's t. 8
Avar Mill t. 9
Avar postern 10

(above) AND CROSS-SECTION (below)
Mr. Pierre EMBRY).

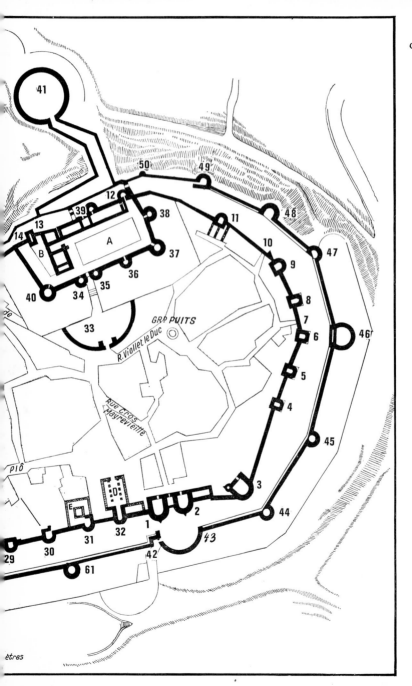

KEY TO THE MAP

THE INNER ENCEINTE.

1 and 2. Narbonnaise Towers.
3. Tresau Tower.
4. Constable's Mill Tower.
5. Vieulas Tower.
6. La Marquiere Tower.
7. The Bourg Doorway.
8. Samson's Tower.
9. The Avar Mill Tower.
10. The Avar Postern.
11. The Charpentiere Tower.
12. The Chapel Tower.
13. The Pinte Tower.
14. The Pinte Postern.
15. The Justice Tower.
16. The Aude Doorway.
17. The Visigothic Tower.
18. The Bishop's Round Tower called the Inquisition Tower.
19. The Bishop's Square Tower.
20. The Cahuzac Tower.
21. The Mipadre Tower.
22. The South Mill Tower.
23. The Saint Nazaire Tower.
24. Saint Martin's Tower.
25. The Prison Tower.
26. The Castera Tower.
27. The Plo Tower.
28. The Balthazar Tower.
29. The Davejean Tower.
30. Saint Laurent Tower.
31. The Trauquet Tower.
32. The Sacraire Saint-Sernin Tower.

CASTLE.

33. The East Barbican.
34 and 35. Towers of the East Doorway.
36. Barracks Tower.

37. The Major's Tower.
38. The Staircase Tower.
39. The Powder Tower.
40. Saint Paul's Tower.
41. The Aude or West Barbican.

THE OUTER ENCEINTE.

42. The Narbonnaise Outer Gateway.
43. The Saint Louis Barbican.
44. The Berard Tower.
45. The Benazet Tower.
46. The Notre-Dame Barbican and postern.
47. The Moreti Tower.
48. The Glaciere Tower.
49. The Red Doorway Tower.
50. The West Bartizan.
51. The Small Canissou Tower.
53. The Big Canissou Tower.
54. The Ourliac Tower.
55. The Grenade Barbican.
56. The Razes Postern.
57. The Cautiere Tower.
58. Pouleto Tower.
59. East Bartizan.
60. La Vade Tower.
61. La Peyre Tower.

MISCELLANEOUS.

A. Great courtyard of the castle.
B. Small courtyard of the castle.
C. Saint-Nazaire Cathedral.
D. Saint Sernin's church (destroyed).
E. The Trauquet Annex (destroyed).

ENGRAVING AND PRINTING
SCOP-SADAG
01200 BELLEGARDE
MCMLXXIII

Legally deposited : 2° quarter 1973
N° of printing : 1067 - N° of edition : 1303

Printed in France